MISSIONS AND
THE AMERICAN MIND

Edition Published for

National Foundation for Education
in
American Citizenship

New York • Indianapolis • Washington

MISSIONS AND THE AMERICAN MIND

By

KENNETH SCOTT LATOURETTE

*D. Willis James Professor of Missions and
Oriental History, Yale University; President,
American Historical Association, 1948*

NATIONAL FOUNDATION PRESS

143 N. Meridian Street, Indianapolis 4

1949

PRINTED IN THE UNITED STATES OF AMERICA

Preface

RELIGION, as a way of life, is the most profound influence in human experience. It imbues plain men with greatness. It endows great men with courage and purpose. And through men's lives the power of the spirit becomes for the nation a foundation and a force for progress.

In the development and preservation of the basic institutions of a free and liberty-loving America, the spiritual power of religion has always played a fundamental part. Free to worship after the dictates of their own consciences, men have woven into the fabric of the republic the dignity and honor of righteousness. The influence of religion in developing the American polity is measured by this series.

The National Foundation for Education in American Citizenship has arranged the Fundamental American Principles Series on Religion to portray for every citizen the contributions of religion to our way of life. Each essay is written by a distinguished authority. The Foundation is a nonpartisan, nonsectarian public trust, and views expressed, as in each of its publications, are those of the author and are not to be interpreted necessarily as views of the Foundation's board or officers.

Topics in the series indicate the breadth and depth of religious influences:

Professor Emeritus of American History, Columbia University

The Churches and the Social Conscience—O. T. Binkley, Professor of Ethics and Sociology, Southern Baptist Theological Seminary

Missions and the American Mind—Kenneth Scott Latourette, D. Willis James Professor of Missions and Oriental History, Yale University

Churches and Education for Practical Democracy—Nelson R. Burr, Library of Congress

Religion and the Civil Liberties—Walter M. Horton, Fairchild Professor of Systematic Theology, Oberlin College

The American Churches in War and Peace—William Warren Sweet, Professor of the History of American Christianity, University of Chicago

The Church and the Democracy of the Future—William Adams Brown, Late Research Professor Emeritus in Applied Theology, Union Theological Seminary

Editors of the series are Frank J. Klingberg, Professor of History, University of California, Los Angeles, and Franklin L. Burdette, Professor of Government and Politics, University of Maryland.

These authoritative summaries show vividly the fundamental relationship between religious faith and basic American principles. The historic role of the churches, the American churches in action, and the role of a nation imbued on the whole with Christian religious standards are treated with understanding and vision. This significant contribution by Professor Latourette was written especially for the series. With the consent of the Foundation and of the editors, it was adapted for publication in *Religion in Life*.

SAMUEL R. HARRELL
Chairman, Board of Trustees
National Foundation for Education
In American Citizenship

vi

Contents

MISSIONS AND THE AMERICAN MIND

Missions and
The American Mind

INTRODUCTION

A CONTINUING and little appreciated factor in the shaping of the American mind has been the Christian missionary enterprise. One of the avowed purposes of the earliest British colonies in what later became the United States was the spread of the Christian faith.

In the fleeting and ill-fated settlement on Roanoke Island there was preaching to the Indians.[1] Both the first and the second charters granted to Virginia, by James I in 1606 and 1609 respectively, formally declared that prominent among the objects of the undertaking was the propagation of the Christian religion.[2] An avowed motive in the founding of the Pilgrim settlement at Plymouth was "a great hope . . . of laying some good foundation . . . for the advancing of the gospel of the kingdom of Christ."[3] The first charter of Massachusetts,

---

[1] J. S. M. Anderson, *The History of the Church of England in the Colonies and the Foreign Dependencies of the British Empire* (London, 1856), Vol. I, pp. 67-71, 74, 75.

[2] See the texts in S. Lucas, *Charters of the Old English Colonies in America* (London, 1850), pp. 2, 18.

[3] *Bradford's History of Plymouth Plantation 1606-1646*, W. T. Davis, editor (New York, 1908), Chapter 2.

which bears the date of 1628, expressed the desire to "win and invite the natives of that country to the knowledge and obedience of the only true God and savior of mankind and the Christian faith."[4]

From these beginnings to the present, the Christian missionary enterprise has been a phase of the life of this country. It has found many expressions. It has endeavored to hold to the Christian faith those who by heredity have been its adherents and to win those who are not professedly Christian, whether they are of European or non-European blood. It has been a companion of the westward-moving frontier of white settlement, proclaiming the Christian message, organizing churches, molding ideals and conduct, and contributing to the spiritual bases of the new commonwealths. It has met the immigrant from Europe, whether on the prairies, in mining and lumber towns, or in great manufacturing and commercial cities, and has built for him churches and schools and has endeavored to confirm him in his ancestral allegiance. It has sought out the non-Christian immigrants from the Far Orient. It has extended its scope to the many Indian tribes which represent the aboriginal population. It has been a powerful force in the life of the American Negroes. It has reached out beyond the borders of the United States and has sent its representatives to every continent and to many of the islands of the sea.

---

[4] Lucas, *op. cit.*, p. 43.

4

Tens of thousands of Americans have gone as missionaries to other countries. They are to be found in all the republics of Latin America, in several of the islands of the Pacific, in many of the political subdivisions of Africa, in some of the countries of Europe, and in most of the nations of Asia. The majority of them have been Protestant but an increasing number are Roman Catholic. Upon the peoples outside the United States they have had marked effects. They have also, and usually in quite unnoticed fashion—through their going, the efforts required to send and maintain them, and their continuing contacts with their home constituencies—contributed to the shaping of the attitudes of hundreds of thousands of Americans.

Any statistical appraisal of the influence of the missionary enterprise on the American mind is impossible. So much is in the realm of the intangibles that it defies exact estimates and at times cannot even be traced to its source. That, we may remind ourselves, is true of other important contributions to the soul of the nation. Enough can be pointed out, even when it cannot be precisely measured, to afford some inkling of the importance of the missionary factor in forming the American mind.

I

WE must note, first of all, the place which the missionary enterprise had in the initial stages of white settlement. Every portion of the United States has had its

5

frontier period. In the older sections of the Thirteen
Colonies the frontier had passed before the United States
came into being. In other regions it persisted down to
the close of the nineteenth century.[5] In a few remote
corners it has continued to this day. The prominence of
the frontier during most of the course of the nation's
life has helped to shape the American spirit. This influence of the frontier has long been recognized by his-
torians. Much of American democracy, with its belief
in the value and basic equality of every person, its self-
reliant individualism, and its dream of giving to all the
opportunity to prove their worth and to share in the
good things of life, goes back to the frontier.

On the frontier, we are told, the social stratifications
and inequalities of Europe and the older settlements
tended to break down. Each man and woman had the
opportunity to display his or her native worth. All were
equal in the sight of the law. This in general was true
of the frontier in the United States. It is very seldom
noted that this was not similarly true of all frontiers of
white settlement. The frontier in the United States dif-
fered in temper from that in French Canada and in Latin
America, although all were in the Western Hemisphere
and both the first two and much of the third were in the
temperate zones. The frontier in the United States con-

---

[5] See the famous study which has become a classic in this field—F. J.
Turner, *The Frontier in American History* (New York, 1920).

tributed much more toward what we term democracy than did the frontier in French, Spanish, and Portuguese America. An important reason for the difference is to be found in the type of Christianity which was propagated.

Much more than in Europe or even in the British Isles, the Christianity of the first stages of the history of the United States was that of the radical wing of the Protestant Reformation. The Protestant Reformation was an extremely varied movement, but it had as one of its dominant characteristics salvation by faith. By this was meant the faith of the individual Christian. As a corollary of salvation by faith there came the right and the duty of private, individual judgment in matters of religion and morals. Each Christian, so this view held, is responsible primarily to God. Neither church nor state must be permitted to come between him and God. All believers are priests. Luther declared that "a Christian man is a perfectly free lord of all, subject to none."[6] Not all the reformers were prepared to push this point to its extreme implications. Luther himself hastened to add that "a Christian man is a perfectly dutiful subject of all, subject to all."[7] He made much of the authority of the state. However, the extremists among the reformers tended to go much further in insisting upon the competence and the duty of the individual Christian to

---

[6] M. Luther, *On Christian Liberty*.
[7] *Ibid.*

judge all institutions. Obviously they were deemed dangerous by the constituted authorities in state and church, whether in Roman Catholic or Protestant lands. Many of them sought refuge in the Thirteen Colonies.

While some of the churches represented in the Thirteen Colonies were those which on the other side of the Atlantic were endorsed by the state and while several of the Thirteen Colonies had an established church, in general the trend was away from this precedent and toward a greater prominence of the left wing of Protestantism. It was this radical form of Protestantism which most multiplied on the frontier. For instance, Baptists, with their individualism and democratic form of church organization, were more characteristic of the frontier than they were of Great Britain. The camp meetings and the revivals through which much of the spread of Christianity on the American frontier was accomplished tended to emphasize individual salvation and worked against conformity to inherited ecclesiastical patterns. More than in Europe and Great Britain or even than on much of the Atlantic seaboard of the United States, it was through the extremely democratic forms of Protestantism that Christianity was propagated on the frontier. Here has been a little appreciated factor in the creation of American democracy. It is, for example, no accident that the hymn *America*, which has done so much to give popular expression to the democracy of the

8

United States, was written by a Baptist clergyman while in his student days. Significantly, in later years he was a secretary of the foreign missionary society of his denomination.[8]

Another important contribution of the missionary enterprise, through its activities on the westward-moving frontier, was in the field of education. Scores of colleges and universities, some of them later among the most important in the country, owed their origin in part or entirely to the missionary impulse. It is a commonplace in the history of American education that the oldest of the universities in the United States, Harvard, was founded on what was then a close approach to the frontier for the purpose of preparing an indigenous clergy to give leadership to the churches when those who had come from England had died. Its charter of 1650, its fundamental source of authority in administration, dedicated the institution to "the education of the English and Indian youth . . . in knowledge and godlynes." Harvard clearly had its roots in the missionary impulse. Similarly William and Mary, the second oldest college in the Colonies, had as its original aim the training of a ministry for the Church in Virginia. One of its professorships was long designated for the teaching of Indians. Princeton traces its inception to the Great Awakening, a missionary movement among the white population, in

---

[8] *Dictionary of American Biography,* Vol. XVII, pp. 342, 343.

part a frontier phenomenon. The University of Pennsylvania dates its beginnings from a charity school inspired by George Whitefield, during part of his life an itinerant missionary in the Thirteen Colonies. Dartmouth College was inaugurated on the then frontier to train missionaries to the Indians.

As the frontier moved westward from the original states along the Atlantic seaboard, its course could be traced by the founding of colleges by religious bodies. Most of these were missionary institutions. They were for the purpose of providing education under Christian auspices for the children of the frontier. Many of them were intimately associated with the home missionary programs of their respective denominations and drew a large part of their original funds from donors in the older states who were impelled by missionary motives.[9] At least three, Illinois College,[10] Iowa (later Grinnell) College,[11] and Whitman College, [12] owed either their inception or much of their foundation to bands of young men who went as missionaries from the older states to the frontier. A single home missionary from New England assisted in founding two colleges on the frontier, one in

---

[9] For an account of many of these see D. G. Tewksbury, *The Founding of American Colleges and Universities before the Civil War with Particular Reference to the Religious Influences Bearing upon the College Movement* (New York, 1932).

[10] *Julian M. Sturtevant, An Autobiography* (New York, 1896), pp. 134-139.

[11] G. F. Magoun, *Asa Turner . . . and His Times* (Boston, 1889), pp. 241 ff.

[12] J. B. Clark, *Leavening the Nation* (New York, 1903), pp. 209-211.

Indiana and one in Oregon.[13] These instances might be multiplied almost indefinitely. Some of the institutions so founded attained great importance. For example, the College of California, inaugurated by the Presbyterians and Congregationalists in the early days of settlement from the older states, was the basis on which later arose the University of California.[14] In several states, among them Michigan,[15] Illinois,[16] South Dakota,[17] and Oregon,[18] the public school systems were deeply indebted to home missionaries.

The moral standards and discipline of the frontier, and of the ensuing communities, owed much to home missionaries and to the churches which they founded. Thus the members of Baptist churches on the frontier covenanted with one another to "exercise a Christian care and watchfulness over each other, and faithfully warn, exhort, and admonish each other as occasion may require." They fulfilled their obligation by actually examining charges against one another of drunkenness, fighting, lying, stealing, irregular sexual relations, malicious gossip, failure to pay just debts, gambling, and horse racing. The obdurately unrepentant might be ex-

---

13 *Correspondence of the Reverend Ezra Fisher* (Portland, Ore., 1916), pp. 58, 281 ff.

14 W. C. Pond, *Gospel Pioneering* (Oberlin, 1921), p. 54.

15 C. B. Goodykoontz, *Home Missions on the American Frontier* (Caldwell, Idaho, 1939), p. 368.

16 Magoun, *op. cit.*, p. 112; Goodykoontz, *op. cit.*, p. 369.

17 *Dictionary of American Biography*, Vol. XIX, pp. 429, 430.

18 *Ibid..* Vol. I, pp. 408, 409.

cluded from church membership.[19] Methodism, also strong on the frontier, by its class system through which its members were given fellowship and supervision in small groups, its local preachers and exhorters, and its structure of circuit riders and conferences, had a marked moral as well as spiritual influence over its members.

Christian missions had a large part in shaping the mind and the spirit of the immigrant. Some of the missionaries to the immigrants were from the Old World. Thus in colonial days Anglicans organized the Society for the Propagation of the Gospel in Foreign Parts[20] and the Society for Promoting Christian Knowledge.[21] Both organizations had the British colonies as their objective and addressed themselves to the white colonists as well as to the Indians and the Negroes. From the Pietist center at Halle, in Germany, came Lutheran missionaries to the German colonists, notably Henry Melchior Muhlenberg. Muhlenberg travelled widely, preaching, admonishing and disciplining those who were guilty of serious moral lapses, and administering the sacraments.[22] In the eighteenth century help was also sent from Eu-

---

[19] W. W. Sweet, *Religion on the American Frontier: The Baptists, 1783-1830* (New York, 1931), pp. 48, 49; R. S. Douglass, *History of Missouri Baptists* (Kansas City, 1934), p. 24.

[20] C. F. Pascoe, *Two Hundred Years of the S. P. G.* (London, 1901), pp. 3-8.

[21] W. O. B. Allen and E. McClure, *Two Hundred Years: The History of the Society for Promoting Christian Knowledge* (London, 1898), pp. 1-24, 61-120.

[22] See especially *The Journals of Henry Melchior Muhlenberg*, translated by T. G. Tappert and J. W. Doberstein (Vol. I., Philadelphia, 1902), *passim*.

rope, in funds and personnel, to the Germans of the Reformed faith.[23] Missionaries from the mother country went to the Germans who migrated in the nineteenth century. Most of them were from theologically conservative and Pietist circles. They helped to nourish that type of mind in those to whom they ministered. They stood for sturdy morals and some of them fostered education.[24] In the early days of the extensive nineteenth century migration of Protestants from Scandinavia there came religious leaders from the home lands to nourish the settlers in their hereditary faith. Some of them were products of the revivals which swept Scandinavia in the nineteenth century and which were in part from Pietistic and in part from Anglo-Saxon contacts. They were strict in morals and helped to give both ethical and spiritual vigor to the Scandinavian communities.[25] Quite rapidly the immigrants set about building their own churches and schools. They bore the chief burden of erecting their own church buildings, recruiting and training their

---

[23] J. H. Dubbs, *History of the Reformed Church, German* (New York, 1895), pp. 255, 278, 279; *Minutes and Letters of the Coetus of the German Reformed Congregations in Pennsylvania, 1747-1792* (Philadelphia, 1903), *passim*.

[24] For some examples, see W. Schlatter, *Geschichte der Basler Mission, 1815-1915* (Basel, 1916), Vol. I, p. 91; C. E. Schneider, *The German Church on the American Frontier* (St. Louis, 1939), pp. 49, 53-58, 91; G. J. Zeilinger, *A Missionary Synod with a Mission* (Chicago, 1929), pp. 7-26, 55-59; *Church History*, Vol. VIII, pp. 222-230.

[25] G. M. Stephenson, *The Religious Aspects of Swedish Immigration* (Minneapolis, 1932), *passim*; O. M. Norlie, *History of the Norwegian People in America* (Minneapolis, 1925), pp. 193-195, 259.

own clergy, and stimulating the organization of new congregations.

The majority of the immigrants of the nineteenth and twentieth centuries were Roman Catholic by heredity. Most of them were from lands where the Roman Catholic Church was closely associated with the state. At first it was a question whether they would build churches and support a body of clergy, for that would have to be done by voluntary contributions and most of them were desperately poor and were having difficulty in establishing themselves in their new homes. It might be that they would drift away from all religion and become a secularized element in American life. That proved to be the case with numbers of them. Most of them and their children, however, remained true to the church of their fathers. For many the connection was nominal. For others it was vital.

The achievement of holding the Roman Catholic immigrants and their children to the faith was, as in the case of Protestants, accomplished in part by assistance from Europe. Many priests, lay brothers, and sisters came from the Old World to serve the settlers in the United States. Here and there in Europe institutions were established specifically for the training of clergy for that country. There was such a one at Münster,[26]

------

[26] T. Roemer, *The Ludwig-Missionsverein and the Church in the United States* (Washington, 1933), p. 50.

another was at Louvain,[27] and still another was in Italy, founded by the Bishop of Piacenza.[28] Fairly large financial subsidies also were sent from Europe. The Society for the Propagation of the Faith, begun in 1822 at Lyons for the purpose of enlisting prayer and money for missions and eventually making itself felt in many lands both as a means of raising money and of providing subsidies for Roman Catholic missions, owed its origin in part to an appeal for aid by a Bishop of New Orleans. It long contributed substantially to the Roman Catholic enterprise in America.[29] The Ludwig-Missionsverein, founded in Bavaria, made the United States its chief beneficiary.[30]

As was the experience of Protestantism, most of the leadership and the funds for holding the Roman Catholic immigrants to the faith were from the United States itself. The achievement was notable. The overwhelming majority of Roman Catholics had low incomes. Out of these in addition to caring for their own families, they built churches and a system of church schools. For many this meant in effect double taxation—such taxes as were collected from them to support the public schools, and fees and contributions which they paid to church insti-

---

[27] *Ibid.*

[28] T. F. Cullen, *The Catholic Church in Rhode Island* (North Providence, R. I., 1936), pp. 362-364.

[29] E. J. Hickey, *The Society for the Propagation of the Faith* (Washington, 1922), pp. 18 ff., 153.

[30] Roemer, *op. cit.*, p. 13.

tutions that their children might have an education in which their faith would be taught concurrently with other subjects. Personnel to staff the churches and schools came increasingly and predominantly from the immigrants and their children.

In general this missionary effort for immigrants who were hereditarily Christian, whether Protestant or Roman Catholic, had two groups of effects upon the American mind. One was the partial perpetuation in the United States of the cultural traditions of the several countries from which the immigrants came. So far as they maintained a church connection—and the large majority seem to have done so—for the most part the immigrants and their children had it with that branch of the Church to which they had been attached in the Old World. Some, both Protestant and Roman Catholic, changed their allegiance and became members of one or another of the churches of the older American stock. Naturally this trend increased in the second and third generations of American-born. Intermarriage, conviction, or social convenience encouraged it. Yet the majority, especially of the immigrants and the first generation of the American-born, held to the particular church of their fathers. Often that church was the chief institution which reminded them of the life of the country of their origin. In its pulpit and, if Protestant, also in the rest of its public services it perpetuated the familiar

16

mother tongue. The church provided a convenient social center for those of the same national background. In the course of time much of the hold-over from the European past faded out. Because of the demand of the second or third generation, the mother tongue was replaced by English, although usually not without a struggle. Roman Catholic parishes made up exclusively of members from one European country diminished. The Roman Catholic Church deliberately set itself against the perpetuation in its organization of Old World differences and insisted upon being American and, so far as that could be done without surrendering its basic and historic teaching and practice, upon becoming identified with the national life. The large Lutheran bodies tended to cling to the national traditions inherited from the Old World, even when English had become the language of the service. The smaller Eastern churches, of which the various branches of the Orthodox were the chief ones, did likewise. The persistence of the different ecclesiastical traditions made for variety in the American scene and the American mind. It led to a much more multiform Christianity than had ever been found elsewhere in the world.

As a corollary, the trend was toward an American Christianity as a feature of the American spirit. This was not by formal ecclesiastical union, although there was some of that within Protestantism. Nor was it being accomplished chiefly by official co-operation among the different bodies, although that increased. It came, rather, by the interpenetration, often almost unnoticed, of the practices and ideals of one religious body by those of another. Most Protestant hymnals drew from authors of many denominational allegiances. The National Conference of Christians and Jews brought together Protestants and Roman Catholics, usually clergymen, as well as Jewish rabbis, for reciprocal understanding. Among the rank and file of laymen the interpenetration was even more marked. Intolerance persisted and occasionally flared forth, but the trend was in the opposite direction. There was no indication that the historic differences which separated Protestants, Roman Catholics, and Orthodox from one another would be erased. Yet, by the association forced by geographic propinquity, a certain community of mind was beginning to emerge to which each of the various traditions contributed.

A second effect of the missionary effort for Christian immigrants was the perpetuation in the American mind of the spiritual and moral traditions of the Christian faith. Much of the movement of the nineteenth and twentieth centuries was in the direction of materialism and secularism. Throughout the Occidental world this was true. The development of science and the application of the findings of science to the meeting of the physical needs of men together with the amazing achievements in manufactures, transportation, and medicine

18

tempted men to assume that their wants could be met in this fashion and that religion was irrelevant. In the United States that tendency was especially strong. The vast natural resources of the land and their large scale exploitation by the facilities provided by the machine made possible undreamed of comfort for hundreds of thousands. It was not strange that men and women were inclined to be absorbed in the rush for wealth and to dream in what appeared to be materialistic terms. The immigrant, uprooted from his ancestral environment, cut off by the Atlantic from his old institutions, dazzled by the possibility of fortune, and pressed by the necessity of making a living under the new conditions, might easily have allowed the Christian faith to drop out of his life. Many did so. The drift was especially strong in those born in the United States. That the secularization was in no small degree offset by idealism was due to what in its largest sense we have called the missionary enterprise. Through the missionary enterprise, indeed, the faith of many was strengthened. For thousands Christianity became less formal and more vital than it had been in the Old World. In Europe, with its state churches, association with the Church was a matter of course. In the United States, where no religion was established by law, church membership was more a matter of individual initiative and choice, and for many took on a deeper significance.

19

There were also Christian missions for some of the immigrants of non-Christian provenance. Most of the hereditary non-Christians were Jews. Very little effort was made by the churches, whether Protestant or Roman Catholic, to reach them.[31] Some Jews became Christians. Many remained with the synagogues of their ancestors or allied themselves with liberal Judaism. The latter appealed more to some among the wealthy and the intelligentsia than to the rank and file. The majority of Jews tended to drift away from all religion and at best preserved only a few of the formal customs of their forebears. For immigrants from the Far East, much less numerous than the Jews, the churches carried on an active missionary enterprise. This was chiefly by the Protestant bodies of the older American stock. Quite a large proportion of the Chinese, Japanese, and Koreans became Christians and were thus brought into conformity with that element of the American mind.[32] In general, moreover, their missionary interest led the churches to espouse the cause of the Orientals against the legal and social discrimination imposed upon them. The missionary forces sought to have the same treatment accorded Orientals in immigration quotas and in naturalization as was given to immigrants from Europe. In the vast dislocation of the Japanese in the Continental United States

---

[31] K. S. Latourette, *A History of the Expansion of Christianity,* Vol. IV (New York, 1941), pp. 292-294, gives a brief summary.

[32] *Ibid.,* pp. 294, 295.

20

following the attack on Pearl Harbor, the missionary agencies labored to ameliorate the lot of the interned and to facilitate their relocation and their assimilation into normal American life.

The Christian missionary enterprise was a potent force in shaping the attitude of white Americans toward the Indians and of helping the Indians to adjust themselves wholesomely to the changed conditions brought by the dominance of the white man and his culture. This was true from the very beginnings of white settlement. Many of the more earnestly Christian colonists sought fair treatment for the Indians. The contention of Roger Williams that the land belonged to the Indians is famous. So, too, are his efforts to prevent wars between Indian tribes and between whites and Indians. The Friends were scrupulous in seeing that the lands acquired by them were sold to them, and willingly, by the Indians.[33] In a famous case which went to the Supreme Court, missionaries submitted to imprisonment to protest the laws enacted by Georgia in derogation of the rights of the Cherokees.[34] For a time, beginning in 1869, in an attempt to improve its service to the Red Man, the Federal Government delegated the nomination of its Indian agents to the various religious bodies engaged in mis-

---

[33] R. W. Kelsey, *Friends and Indians* (Philadelphia, 1917), pp. 23, 24.

[34] R. S. Walker, *Torchlights of the Cherokees* (New York, 1931), pp. 256-307.

sions.[35] There were Christian missions to most of the Indian tribes. They were sent by Roman Catholics, Protestants, and Russian Orthodox. Most of them were by the first two branches of the Church. These missions began in early colonial days and have continued to the present. In their earlier stages they included the famous Spanish Roman Catholic enterprises in what are now the southern portions of the country from Florida and Georgia to California,[36] the notable French Roman Catholic activities in the Mississippi Valley,[37] the Russian Orthodox efforts in Alaska, and the many Protestants along the Atlantic seaboard from John Eliot on the outskirts of Boston, the Mayhews on Martha's Vineyard, to the Moravians in Pennsylvania and Ohio, and the agents of the Society for the Propagation of the Gospel in Foreign Parts.[38] In the nineteenth and twentieth centuries they ranged from the Atlantic to the Pacific and from the extreme South to the extreme North.[39] They sought to win the Indians to the Christian faith and conducted schools for them. In the inevitable process of assimilation of these scattered racial minorities to the culture of the dominant white man, Christian missions embodied the idealism of the American mind and so

---

[35] L. F. Schmeckebier, *The Office of Indian Affairs* (Baltimore, 1927), pp. 54, 55.

[36] Latourette, *op. cit.*, Vol. III, pp. 125-132.

[37] *Ibid.*, pp. 180-182.

[38] *Ibid.*, pp. 216-224.

[39] See a summary, with appropriate references, *ibid.*, Vol. IV, pp. 299-324.

22

helped to implant in the Indian that phase of the civilization to which he was conforming.

Much more numerous than the Indians were the Negroes. As in the case of the Indians, the missionary enterprise taken in its broadest sense both contributed to the attitudes of the white man toward the Negro and assisted the Negro in making a wholesome adjustment to the culture into which he had been involuntarily thrust and to acquire the idealistic and religious features of the American mind. The Christian conscience was the chief source of the movements to better the lot of the Negro, first through emancipation and then through education. As early as 1693 the Friends' Philadelphia Yearly Meeting advocated the emancipation and education of the slaves owned by its members.[40] In the last quarter of the eighteenth century the Philadelphia Yearly Meeting determined to exclude from membership all who declined to free their slaves.[41] Religious revivals, which in America have been missionary movements to reach those not as yet Christian and to give fresh vigor to the faith of those already Christian, were fruitful sources of impulses to emancipate the Negro slaves. In 1776 Samuel Hopkins, an exponent of the Great Awakening and in the spiritual succession of Jonathan Edwards, asked the Continental Congress to abolish slavery.[42] David Rice,

---

[40] L. A. Weigle, *American Idealism* (New Haven, 1928), p. 161.
[41] *Ibid.*
[42] *The Works of Samuel Hopkins,* Vol. II, pp. 549 ff.

an indefatigable evangelist and one of the earliest Presbyterian ministers in Kentucky, strove for the gradual emancipation of slaves in that state.[43] Barton W. Stone, another leader of the revivals in Kentucky, freed his slaves.[44] The great revivals in the first half of the nineteenth century associated with the name of Charles G. Finney gave a marked impetus to the anti-slavery movement. One of the Finney converts, Theodore Dwight Weld, was a flaming missionary and organizer of the movement.[45] Out of the revivals came Lyman Beecher. One of his daughters, Harriet Beecher Stowe, was the author of *Uncle Tom's Cabin,* the most potent literary contribution to emancipation.

The missionary agencies of the white churches contributed significantly to the education of the Negro. Indeed, at the outset practically all the secondary and higher schools for Negroes were their creation. Even today a very large proportion of the best colleges and universities for Negroes are those founded by these agencies. To them have been added in the course of the years others, some of them the creation of the Negro churches and some of them supported by public funds. Simply to list a few of the outstanding colleges and uni-

---

[43] Asbury, Apr. 10, 1792, in *The Heart of Asbury's Journal* (New York, 1904), p. 334; *Dictionary of American Biography,* Vol. XV, pp. 537-538.

[44] A. W. Fortune, *The Disciples of Kentucky* (The Convention of the Christian Churches in Kentucky, 1932), p. 44.

[45] G. H. Barnes, *The Anti-Slavery Impulse* (New York, 1933), *passim.*

versities which were begun by white missionary agencies is, to any one familiar with even the barest outlines of Colored education, to show the part which the missionary spirit played in training Negro leaders. The American Missionary Association was the parent of Hampton Institute, whose chief creator, Samuel Chapman Armstrong, was the son of a missionary to Hawaii[46] and whose most famous graduate, Booker T. Washington, was in turn the main force in the birth and growth of Tuskegee.[47] From the American Missionary Association also came Fisk University, Atlanta University, Talladega College, Tougaloo University, Straight University, and Tillotson College.[48] Spelman College, the most noted higher school for Negro women, was the creation of the Woman's American Baptist Home Mission Society and the American Baptist Home Mission Society.[49] Howard University had its inception in a prayer meeting in the First Congregational Church of Washington, D. C.[50] The place of the Christian missionary forces in the inauguration of education, and especially of higher education, for Negroes witnesses to one of the deep-seated convic-

---

[46] E. A. Talbot, *Samuel Chapman Armstrong* (New York, 1904), *passim.*

[47] Booker T. Washington, *Up from Slavery* (New York, 1901), *passim; Booker T. Washington's Own Story of His Life and Work* (Naperville, 1916), *passim.*

[48] *Twenty-Ninth Report of the American Missionary Association* (1875), p. 76. *Fifty-Sixth Annual Report of the American Missionary Association* (1902), p. 15.

[49] P. M. Whipple, *Negro Neighbors Bond and Free* (Boston, 1907), pp. 122 ff.

[50] D. O. W. Holmes, in *The Journal of Negro History*, Vol. III, pp. 131 ff.

tions of the Christian missionary enterprise—the infinite worth of every human soul, the capacity of all men, no matter of what race, for spiritual and mental development, and their right to opportunity for that growth. This faith in the potentialities of individuals of all races was especially characteristic of the extreme wing of Protestantism which was prominent in the United States. That element in the American mind which has been most active in inspiring and sustaining efforts for the legal and social emancipation of the Negroes and for opening to them opportunities for spiritual, intellectual, and social development is at least largely, and is probably predominantly, the product of the missionary impulse. The confidence and the devotion with which many Negroes have labored for these goals for members of their own race also are in part from this same source.

In the course of their sojourn in the United States, and especially after emancipation, the American Negroes have been extensively permeated by Christianity. The American Negro mind is to a considerable degree the creation of Christian missions. Approximately as large a proportion of Negroes as of whites are members of churches. Some of the spread of Christianity among the Negroes has been due to the efforts of white Christians, particularly in pre-emancipation days. More of it has been through the efforts of the Negroes themselves. The overwhelming majority of Negro Christians have been

Protestants. This seems to have been because the religious contacts of the Negroes have been chiefly with Protestants. Except in Louisiana Roman Catholics have not been prominent in the states which have been the traditional home of most of the Colored people. Of the Protestant denominations the Baptists and Methodists have made the chief appeal to the Negroes. The overwhelming majority of Negro Christians have been in these two religious families. This fact seems to be associated with the extensive spread of the Baptists and Methodists among the lower income and social strata of the older white American stock—the elements in the white population most akin in their intellectual and social outlook to the Negroes. Because the missionary methods of the Baptists and Methodists were best adapted to winning what may in a somewhat loose fashion be described as the proletariat of the older American white population, they succeeded among the Negroes. The extreme democracy of the Baptist organization has helped to nourish democracy in the Negro mind and institutions. The Methodist passionate conviction that all men can, if they will but accept the way freely offered by God in Christ, be saved and become children of God has also given dignity to the Negro soul. The emotionalism of the methods by which both Baptists and Methodists prosecuted their mission in approaching the whites struck a responsive chord in the Negro heart. Negro Christianity has in turn contributed to the nation as a whole through its "spirituals." Many of these spirituals were inspired by white prototypes, but in the forms in which they became known the country over they were essentially Negro creations.[51]

II

THUS FAR we have been speaking of the effect of what might be called "domestic" missions. What are usually termed "foreign" missions have also had a marked even though a still less easily measured effect upon the American mind.

Since at least the beginning of the nineteenth century the outlook of the missionarily minded has tended to be global. It has embraced all mankind. Samuel J. Mills, who in the first two decades of the nineteenth century was one of the most creative spirits in the American missionary enterprise, is said to have declared to one of his friends, "though you and I are very little beings, we must not rest satisfied till we have made our influence extend to the remotest corner of this ruined world."[52] In his own person Mills did much to embody that ideal. In his brief life (he died in his middle thirties), he was one of the moving spirits in the creation of the American Board of Commissioners for Foreign Missions, he helped to in-

---

[51] G. P. Jackson, *White Spirituals in the Southern Uplands* (Chapel Hill, N. C., 1933), pp. 242 ff.

[52] G. Spring, *Memoirs of the Rev. Samuel J. Mills* (New York, 1820), p. 25.

itiate steps which later led to a mission to Hawaii, he made two journeys to the then frontier in the Mississippi Valley, he dreamed of a tour to South America to open that continent to Protestant missions, and he died while on a trip to Africa which issued in the founding of Liberia.[53]

Throughout the nineteenth century the world outreach of Christianity was the dream of those most concerned for missions. In the latter part of the century a group of young men gave it phrasing in what became the watchword of the Student Volunteer Movement for Foreign Missions—"the evangelization of the world in this generation."[54] By this was not intended the winning of all the world to the Christian faith in a generation, still less the Christianization of the world in one lifetime. It declared, rather, that each generaton of Christians has the obligation to give to all their contemporaries the world around the opportunity to hear the Christian message. Under the inspiration of the watchword tens of thousands of young men and women from the colleges and theological seminaries of the United States "volunteered" for foreign missions and thousands of them actually became missionaries in other lands. From the United States the movement spread to Protestant circles in other lands and with the same watchword.

---

[53] Spring, *op. cit.*, pp. 47 ff., 59 ff., 102 ff., 132 ff.
[54] Robert P. Wilder, *The Great Commission* (London, 1936), *passim.*

Some of the leading spirits in the Student Volunteer Movement for Foreign Missions, notably John R. Mott, were active, in the 1890's, in the formation of the World's Student Christian Federation,[55] and, in the next century, of the International Missionary Council[56] and the World Council of Churches. In other words, through their missionary purpose and vision Americans were helping to create among Protestant Christians a world-embracing fellowship which was holding out friendly hands to Christians of eastern churches and, so far as the traditional gulf would allow, to Roman Catholics. That fellowship arose from the purpose of bringing the Christian message to the entire world and had among its objectives the permeating of all mankind with Christian ideals. It talked of "world conquest," but by that it meant not political or even cultural subjugation, still less ecclesiastical imperialism. It sought to bring into being the world around self-governing, self-supporting, self-propagating churches which would be knit together with other churches in all lands on the basis of equality. More and more there arose into positions of prominence in the World's Student Christian Federation and the International Missionary Council Christians from non-European peoples. It became a matter of pride that at the meeting of the International Missionary Council, held in Ma-

---

[55] C. P. Shedd, *Two Centuries of the Student Christian Movements* (New York, 1934), pp. 355 ff.

[56] B. Mathews, *John R. Mott* (London, 1934), pp. 220 ff.

dras in 1938, non-Occidental delegates approximately equalled in numbers those from Occidental lands.

This movement was predominantly Protestant. Until the second decade of the present century American Roman Catholics were so engrossed in the urgent task of providing clergy, churches, and schools for the millions of their faith who were pouring across the Atlantic that they had little energy to spare for other countries. When, beginning with the World War of 1914-1918, a drastic reduction of immigration gave them opportunity to catch up with their domestic tasks and some of their number who had been longer in the New World began to share in the riches of the land and to rise above the lower income levels, American Roman Catholics began also to reach out to other parts of the world. Through the very organization of their church, which places the word Catholic, or universal, to the fore, and which extends to almost every people, American Roman Catholics have an inducement to a world outlook. It has been somewhat slower to develop than among Protestants, but latterly it has had a striking growth.

The effect of this world-wide missionary enterprise upon the American mind is seldom appreciated. Even those most active in it are infrequently aware of how deeply it has molded the American outlook on the world. The supporting constituency of foreign missions numbers millions. Literally millions contribute financially to the enterprise. Not many of them give a large proportion of their income. To most of them foreign missions are a minor interest. Yet to a substantial minority, numbering thousands, they are a major concern. Nearly every Protestant congregation has, under one name or another, its missionary society. Each of these has its officers, usually women. This interest is not selfish. Of the millions who give to the support of missions and of the thousands who go as missionaries, very few have any desire for the aggrandizement of themselves or of the United States. Indeed, a very large proportion of American missionaries are in countries or regions, such as India, the Near East, and the Belgian Congo, where the United States has no political foothold and, until recently in the Near East, comparatively unimportant commercial contacts. In the Far East, where American missionaries are particularly prominent, American political and commercial stakes are large, but few of the supporters of the first have as a motive the reinforcement of the other two phases of American activity.

Accompanying the missionary enterprise is an extensive education of the supporting constituency. In part this is through addresses and sermons by missionaries on furlough, by secretaries of mission boards, or by other informed advocates. In part it is through periodicals. In part it is through textbooks designed for reading or for classes of various age groups. The periodicals are usually sold for a small subscription price and some of them have a circulation of several thousands. Through the textbooks tens of thousands are reached each year. Many of the texts are undenominational. For instance, the Missionary Educational Movement serves a number of Protestant bodies. Each year it devotes its books to a particular area or type of work and has books for the several ages from the primary grades to adults. In the aggregate its books are probably read by at least a hundred thousand persons a year. In addition, several of the denominations prepare textbooks of their own. Some of the addresses and the periodicals stress the seamy side of the cultures to which missionaries go. By so doing they would portray the need and elicit sympathy and support. Particularly in later decades, the text books and the periodicals present favorable as well as unfavorable aspects of other lands. The typical mission study book begins with a well rounded description of the country which is its subject. It tells of the geography, the natural resources, the history, the culture, and the current problems. As a rule the account is sympathetic and, if it departs from full objectivity, errs on the side of sympathy with the people whom it portrays. It then goes on to an account of the missionary enterprise in that land, its achievements and its needs. Some of these books contain the best brief accounts of a land and its contemporary status to be found in the English language.

Through this missionary education thousands of Americans have obtained almost their sole knowledge of other peoples. For thousands of others it has been one of their sources. Secretary Henry L. Stimson declared: "The most widespread interest of our people in China is not commercial. . . . Our most general information of China has come through. . . . the great missionary movement—religious, educational and medical—which has been carried on in China for nearly a century by the churches and humanitarian interests of this country."[57] Wendell L. Willkie bore independent testimony of the same tenor when he said: "Back in my home town in Indiana when I was a boy, we were always raising funds for foreign missions. Our Sunday schools provided us with books on foreign lands written by returning missionaries. They stimulated our interest in foreign countries."[58]

Through the missionary enterprise have come some of the American scholars who have contributed to the solid foundation of expert knowledge of other lands. This contribution to scholarship has been notable in the case of China. Most of the prominent American sinologists have been missionaries or the children of missionaries. The outstanding American sinologist of the second half of the nineteenth century was S. Wells Williams,

---

[57] H. L. Stimson, *The Far Eastern Crisis* (New York, 1936), p. 153.
[58] Address to the Presbyterian General Assembly, Detroit, May 31, 1943.

who first went to China as a missionary.[59] His *The Middle Kingdom* was long the best comprehensive treatment of China in the English Language and his *A Syllabic Dictionary of the Chinese Language* remains the best of its kind produced by an American. When, in 1928, the American Council of Learned Societies set up its Committee on the Promotion of Chinese Studies, the original membership, supposedly the outstanding sinologists in the country, was more than half of missionaries, former missionaries, or children of missionaries. The majority of the chairmen of the committee have been of that category.

Because of the prominence of China as a land to which American missionaries have gone, the knowledge of that country in the United States owes a peculiar debt to them. However, the insights into other lands brought to Americans through the missionary enterprise has by no means been limited to that country. South America, the Near East, India, Burma, Ceylon, the Philippines, Korea, Japan, and much of Africa would be far less known by great masses of Americans were it not for the missionary.

The missionary enterprise has, then, been an important agency in educating Americans in world-mindedness. Through planning in terms of "the evangelization

---

59 F. W. Williams, *The Life and Letters of Samuel Wells Williams* (New York, 1889), *passim*.

of the world in this generation" it has taught thousands to think in global terms. By its very nature it has been anti-isolationist. It has helped to familiarize thousands of Americans with country after country and people after people with whom they would otherwise have little or no direct contact.

Even more significantly, the missionary enterprise has contributed a particular kind of world-mindedness. It has encouraged thousands of Americans to think of the rest of the world not as a field for political or commercial empire but as an opportunity for brotherhood. For more than forty years, in the closing decade of the nineteenth century and the opening decades of the twentieth century, the Student Volunteer Movement for Foreign Missions brought together at its quadrennial conventions more students from more different colleges and universites in the United States than did any other gatherings. At one of these, held soon after the World War of 1914-18, the hymn most frequently sung had among its lines: "Not with swords, loud clashing, or roll of stirring drums; with deeds of love and mercy the heavenly kingdom comes." At another, held a few years later, when the clouds which later broke in the World War of 1939 were palpably gathering, a hymn repeatedly sung declared: "In Christ there is no East or West, in Him no South or North, but one great fellowship of love throughout the whole wide earth." Whether or not these hymns reflect an idealism impossible of full realization, the fact remains that through the movement to which they provided slogans they nurtured in a substantial minority of Americans the conviction that the world is one, that Christians must think in terms of the entire globe and not of any one country or segment, that that world should be a brotherhood all of whose members should unselfishly assist one another, and that it is the duty and the privilege of Christians to help bring that world into the realm of reality. As a foreshadowing of what that world might be, representatives of the best of other races—Negroes from Africa and from the United States, Chinese, Japanese, Indians, and others—were brought to the platforms of these student and other missionary gatherings to speak on behalf of their respective peoples. Books written sympathetically about their own peoples by citizens of other countries were widely circulated.[60] Textbooks on the problem of race as a world issue, presenting generous views of other peoples and suggesting concrete solutions for interracial tensions were prepared and widely studied.[61] After the outbreak of the World War of 1939, a book which sold more than fifty thousand copies was circulated among students and churches ad-

---

[60] See the series, *Christian Voices around the World,* edited by M. T. Stauffer (New York, 7 vols., 1927).

[61] Outstanding among these was R. E. Speer, *Race and Race Relations: A Christian View of Human Contacts* (New York, 1924).

37

vocating world order from the standpoint of all mankind as the family of God.[62]

The type of world-mindedness inculcated by the missionary enterprise may seem to some to ignore the hard facts of life. To speak of the "whole wide earth" becoming "one fellowship of love" appears to ignore the crass and aggressive selfishness which are chronic and at times rampant. Without seeking either to defend or to challenge that attitude, one must point out three related facts of the missionary attitude. Those who have taken it have been aware of human frailty and have called it by a stronger word, sin. To Mills and his fellows it was a "ruined world" to which they were called to go.[63] Yet they were convinced that in the Christian Gospel was the "good news" of power to meet and overcome sin. Inspired by that belief, tens of thousands of Americans have given their lives, many of them in difficult situations in the United States, and others in the various lands beyond the borders of the United States.

III

IN the Christian missionary enterprise has been one of the potent factors shaping the American mind. It has contributed to the view that every man, whether in the

---

[62] R. P. Barnes, *A Christian Imperative: Our Contribution to World Order* (New York, 1941).

[63] See this attitude of American Protestantism developed in H. R. Niebuhr, *The Kingdom of God in America* (Chicago, 1937), *passim*.

United States or in any other country of the world, is of infinite worth, and that this worth is irrespective of color, race, or class. It has taught that there is at the heart of the universe, and governing it, One Who is seeking to lift all men out of the sad condition in which they find themselves to a life, both now and hereafter, of undreamed richness of spirit, a life lived in love and adoration of God and in respect and love for all other men. It has declared it to be the duty of every Christian to work for the realization of that ideal and has held that when one so gives himself he has the assistance of infinite power—power which expressed itself once in time upon a cross. This element in the American mind is by no means dominant. Yet it must be reckoned with by anyone who would understand the United States. It has made itself felt and continues to do so not only in what is usually called the religious realm but also in movement after movement for social reform, both domestic and worldwide. In the domestic scene it has contributed to such movements as the emancipation and advancement of the Negro, the protection of the Indian, and the struggle for greater opportunity for all the underprivileged. On the worldwide scene it has been one of the chief sources—historically, indeed, the original impulse—of the movement for world peace and world organization. It has sought to fight disease, ignorance, vice, and the exploitation of man by his fellows in every quarter of the globe. At times it has seemed to be a waning factor. Yet on a worldwide scale it has had its most extensive expressions in the present century. It is planning hopefully for the decades ahead. It knows that these are to be stormy, but, in the words of one of the most influential of the American leaders of the missionary enterprise of the past four or five decades, paraphrasing the words of a great missionary of the first century of the Christian era, it believes that where sin, national and international, has abounded, grace can much more abound.